Go Find Less

Katrina Helen Childs

Go Find Less © 2022 Katrina Helen Childs

All rights reserved.

No part of this publication may be reproduced, stored in a retrieval system, or transmitted, in any form or by any means, electronic, mechanical, photocopying, recording or otherwise, without the prior written permission of the presenters.

Katrina Helen Childs asserts the moral right to be identified as author of this work.

Presentation by *BookLeaf Publishing*

Web: www.bookleafpub.com

E-mail: info@bookleafpub.com

ISBN: 9789395413718

First edition 2022

DEDICATION

To the people who love me unconditionally and taught me what real love looks like

Your love, support and encouragement gets me through everything

ACKNOWLEDGEMENT

Thank you to everyone who has ever loved me, hurt me or taught me a lesson in life. You're the reason I wrote these poems, and how I was able to grow into the person I am.

PREFACE

My poems are my journal. I process my emotions by writing poetry and using them to decipher what I feel and how to deal with my situation. This collection of poems are some of my most raw entries, that I wrote during the hardest times of my adult life in the past three years.

1/18/2019 10:02 AM

You are soft
The sunshine that peeks beneath the curtain of
the first room I've ever rented
The way my sheets feel on my skin after I've
shaved my legs for the first time in weeks
The kisses you plant on my face when I'm
asleep, as to not wake me

You are strong
The hand I hold when I falter
The demons you fight for yourself and for me

You are weak
The tears that fall late at night- for no one else to
see
The insecurities that I allow myself to have
when you want me to bare my all to you

You are love
The feeling in my chest that makes me want to
burst
The nicknames, late nights, beautiful moments
Your smile and the sound of your voice
Your downfalls and your successes

You are everything.

That is what I am most thankful for.
You are everything
And because of that
You are everything to me

8/21/2019 11:57 AM

Your scent lingered on my hands
I can still feel them on the back of your neck
Your cheeks
The small of your back

It did not take long for your scent to wash away
I must have inhaled every bit of you that I could
Reveled in your hands on the side of my face
In my hair
Between my legs

The last squeeze of my hand before you changed
your mind
The last pained look into my eyes
Before you were down the stairs
And out the front door

I prayed you would come back up.
That you would touch me once more.
I knew it wouldn't happen.
But I waited.
And waited.
Until exhaustion took over me

I wake up alone

With traces of you lingering all over me
And my room
And my life

8/23/2019 7:08 PM

Your hands
Run over my body
Feeling like a warm summer breeze
Pushing its way through my clothes
Making me pause to breathe it in

This feeling
Makes me want to be attached to you
So I can always feel that warm breeze
Against my naked skin

But is it the warm breeze that I cherish
Or is it your hands

Gentle and curious
Running your fingers up and down my arms
Before our eyes have opened for the day
Wishing we didn't have to separate
And pull our bodies from your sheets

What I would have given
To have stayed that way with you

9/3/2019 11:24 AM

I do not want this anymore
The indecisiveness
Having to wake up every morning with
obligation
My body weighed down by the sand under my
skin

I am tired
From fighting day after day
For happiness
For money
For worth

I just want to lie in the grass
And decompose
Become one with the earth
And known I am beautiful
Know I am doing something worthwhile

Knowing I have a purpose

9/29/2019 9:43 PM

One day I will feel again.

The scorpion inside me will defrost
And sting my heart
Lighting again the fire inside it
Sparking inspiration
Determination

The walls will not be walls
They will be gusts of wind
Carrying me to who I am meant to be
And who is meant to love me

I will be able to return that love
Passionately and fully
Truly and openly

The pain has weakened my poor scorpion heart
In such a way that I do not know who I am
And that I have forgotten my most basic instinct
How to love

I have been terrified
That I will not feel it again
I will stay dull like an old penny

Never once shining in any sort of light

I am begging you
Polish me

10/3/2019 2:57 PM

My whole goddamn life
I've been told I'm "too much"
It took me a long time to climb that wall
To forget I was annoying to some
And accept myself

But then you came.
With your false gods
And slick words
And made me forget as well

Until one day it was too much again.
I wanted to see you too much.
I talk too much.
I love my friends too much.

Do you know what this has done to me?
I cannot speak without heavily thinking about
what I'm saying first
I cannot send a message
Or answer the phone
Or fucking sing
Without thinking "is this too much?"

How dare you tell me

I am too much
No one ever tells the sun
It shines too much
That is what I am- I am the sun
And I feel sad for you
That you couldn't see how brightly I shine
And appreciate it fully

Now I am left with my brightness
Inside myself
Stifled by fear of "too much"

12/6/2020 5:15 PM

I had
Every opportunity
To do to you
Exactly what you did to me
People
Falling in line
Propositions
Offers
Escape routes
All because they
Just wanted to feel my heat
The warmth of the way I glow
The same glow I had
For you
But I stayed loyal
Because commitment
And love mean something more to me
Than they obviously mean to you

-Fuck you

I glow brighter without you

12/30/2020 10:11 PM

Not until the flowers grow through my bones
Will I be enough for hands such as yours
To reach down and caress my petals
Gently, full of love

The way your hands on my face feel
Is familiar and gentle, but intentional
You radiate toward me
We envelope each other with soft touch

The whispers in the night
Land softly on my ears, like a drizzle on my
leaves
Loosening my bones and inhibitions
Greasing up the chains that keep me in my
self-dug grave

Allowing me to slowly
But surely
Come to the surface
A new set of bones in a new world

3/20/2021 11:56 AM

I always deserved
So much more
Than you could give me

Thank you for doing me the service of leaving
So I could find someone worthy of my time
Who appreciates my laugh
And doesn't shy away from my feelings

I would have never known happiness
If you hadn't made the choice to leave me
Crying on a street corner
Surrounded by people you don't know

My life has changed for the better
Tenfold
Since you've been gone
A weight has lifted off my chest
It feels like I've been set free
That I can truly be myself without fear of
reaction
Because that is me and I cannot change it
You suppressed my shine
And now act like you support hers

Only because I told you what you had done to
me

5/10/2021 10:37 AM

"You feel like home"
The amount of times
I've longed for you the past 30 months
Confirms it-
You feel like home, too.

So many days
Longing for your smile
A deep hug, full of emotion at 3 am
To hear you asking for me once more

I would have given anything to be exactly where
we are right now
Simply communicating, civilly
This?
This is more than I ever expected or could have
asked for
But it's also everything I've been missing
Everything I've ever wanted
It just feels
So damn good to be
Home.

5/13/2021 11:52 AM

We were just kids at 19
Making plans for big things
That we didn't know the reality behind
Dreaming of life together
That optimism is what brought us to love
The loss of that is what drove us apart

I hope that now we have realistic expectations
Of what the world is like
Maybe that can bring us back
To that love we once had
Because I can still feel it in my bones
It's deep rooted enough
That the only way it would ever go away
Is to replace each bit of my skeleton
Piece by piece

The only way
To rid me of you
Is to change who I am entirely

Unrealistic

6/28/2021 11:42 PM

I stare at you
Drinking in every bit of your profile
The way your nose turns up just a bit
A sparkle every time you smile
Meticulously placed freckles that line your
cheeks
You were made by something miraculous
Forces I don't quite understand

Without a warning, you're looking back at me
Studying me the same way
I had just been to etch you in my memory
Those green eyes overtake me
Wrapping me in your gaze
A swelling in my chest
A smile creeps to my lips involuntarily
I've never seen something quite as beautiful
As you

7/1/2021 2:23 PM

The things I would do to be yours
Could be considered immoral
I'd tear my heart out of my chest
With bare hands
Just to present it to you
To prove I am for you only

I have never craved someone
So violently
The magic that explodes when your fingers
touch my flesh
Takes my breath away
Leaving me dizzy

I want to be bold now
To tell you every single thing my heart feels
Open up in ways I thought I never could
Tearing through the scar tissue of the past
Ask you if you want to be mine
To continue this cosmic connection
That the moon laid out for us
Say the word-
A simple yes
And I'll take you with me

9/16/2021 3:34 PM

I let the feeling of the storm
Overtake me
Soaking me to my core
Chilling my bones
Washing me clean of tragedy
Rinsing off the residue of hands that touched me
who didn't deserve to
The reminder of their pain dripping down my
skin
To the ground
I let the drops remind me
I am free
I am not defined by what has been done to me

9/21/2021 12:52 PM

Surrounded by water
In public but alone
From the game we played
You drew a card
"How many times have you been in love?"
You said none
And I said one
By the time we parted the next day
My answer was two

My answer is still two

11/19/2021 1:04 PM

I awake suddenly from a dream of you
The first in months
To a bed that isn't empty
But you're still not here

You were here
3 weeks ago
Hands on my face and in my hair
Giving me hope for the future
Making me feel alive for the first time in months
But today the lips that kissed me goodbye were
not yours

My god I wish they were yours

I start my day with a chest full of pain
Until today I could stave it off
Fight it for a few hours until I'm not longer
distracted
Today the wave has overtaken me
All I can feel is the losing fight I have with
holding back tears

Why did I deserve this?

11/29/2021 12:49 PM

I rinse you off me
For the last time
Throw the photos out that never should have
been framed
Give away clothes that shouldn't have been left
Remove any trace of your existence from my
phone
Unfollowing and unfriending
Deleting backups and backups of backups
I am so tired of waiting for someone to realize
they want me
I want me
I want to be happy
I choose to be happy

1/21/2022 2:47 PM

I wish I had known
That you existed in the world
That you would melt all of my walls
With a single look
That had the fervor to terrify a forest

I never knew
I could touch someone for the first time
And it would rock the foundation
Of everything I've known to be love

I've always wondered
Why people chased love
If it always ended with third degree burns
Down in flames, alone in the ashes
Sore and raw to the touch

But now I know
The truth is in your fingertips brushing my skin
Behind your breath on my neck
Swimming in the depths of the way you look at
me
Like I could rearrange your universe
With a simple nod

2/25/2022 6:35 PM

It's easy to feel inconsequential
When people can walk out of your life with ease
No regrets
No looking back
I cannot count on both hands
How many people quickly became strangers
Because I was so unimportant in their lives
That it did not matter if I existed on their
timeline
As if their plane of existence saw me as a blip
An anomaly that didn't belong
So it removed me
Allowing them to move on to what they belong
to

"You."

Plainly said in the car
When asked who your first love was
But the effect it had on my universe
The cosmos burst with the pressure of what they
had been missing
The stars aligned us together again
My heart burst in my chest
Making it hard to breathe
All I could do was stare
Until you smiled at me

6/20/2022 6:39 PM

Desperately trying to remind myself
Of how good and free it felt to love so fully
To forget how small and scared I feel now
Terrified of starting again

Because why set myself up for more hurt?
Why look toward something that may never
exist for me?
Hasn't love only left me more lonely?

But I grasp at beautiful memories
Of the wind in my hair
Waking in the night, wrapped around the one I
love
A hand to hold when things get difficult
Someone that makes the future seem bright

The little things that make the hurt
The fear
The pain of trying again and again
So worth it